A Snowfire Not Born(e) Again

Matthew Goethe

Sweet Wreath
Irondale, Alabama

A Snowfire Not Born(e) Again
By Matthew Goethe

©2022 Sweet Wreath
First Edition
All rights reserved
Printed in USA

Designed by Jasper Lee

Goethe, Matthew
A Snowfire Not Born(e) Again
ISBN: 978-1-7368692-1-5
Library of Congress Control Number: 2022915676

A Snowfire Not Born(e) Again

Contents

Inheritance 11
Orthonographic crosshatch 12
two sheets 14
Sin qua non 16
Mezzaluna 17
Nasturtium Falls 21
Paducah 22
The charter 23
Marbles will leave you on the stairs 24
Dryheel (Pearl) 26
Sister among the bulls 28
Ovum 1 29
Ovum 2 30
Ovum 4 31
Robert Hays Segraves 32
Afterword 35
Beth-Salem 39
[an overlapping] 40
[an analogical patience...] 41
[binding of the mouth freelances...] 42
Stethoscope in Garden 43
Copy of *Ukπu O c t p g t* 45
Silver changes hands 47
War 49
Open window 50
I hear an animal that is not singing 51
A snowfire not born(e) again 53
Photograph of silo and Nora Leintz 61
Ensiform 62

Artifacts of the human dead 63
Place de la Révolution 64
Dehiscence 65
Dear _____ 67
Herr Night blows the dinner whistle 68
The work of night is coming 69
[...] 70
If I could tell you how to isolate things 71

For my father

Words decompose you
By mistranslating your mistranslated death
Words decompose death

Inheritance

water laughs and doesn't laugh
fetal inch turns between partitioned locks of highways
legs

hours all end in r's
water laughs and doesn't laugh

eyelash rises and doesn't rise
pools dark eye vials where you
are just a hand fear cannot deter

bridges hung with harpoons
finishing finishes and doesn't finish
why not harps?
we cannot take that chance

what would be our live stock?
dry bones in a barrel
make a barrel of dry bones

doesn't this relate
to an infected mosquito bite
like countries' coalescences
of somnambulant blood
wars leaking a perfumed
relocation of forests that were
taken as the breath of stars
we put in bridges

no, I won't swear on the left testicle
that you never had guts
not to swear on

embryonic leaf twists the water
and as vanishing vanishes and doesn't vanish
the river turns over

Orthogonagraphic crosshatch

spine emarginated
      leaves caught blood in borders
sawing at the sewing
    gone on in
        magma printed
      miner's fingers

white flower emanates
      some thing doored
    red   white-eared
    proud flesh
    propitiation holding a level
        up to despair
diagonal crucible

        pendant swing
    contains shoulder of
      girasol
a poem that is a cyclone
    above itself

have some?

buzzards' motorcycle breathing
shakes wooden jar in its
    own temples
for some incumbent
a recompense
      needed
because they
thought it wasn't there

there are blinds over all
    the pockets
if you can find them
    they will be of use
if you cannot

they will not be needed
how do the dead call
      us?
how do they define a cell?

where should the pulpit
be if not in the fireplace?
not underlined
     or underlied

    these are barriers,
          barterers, barkers,
pointers, men with umbrellas
the sanctions against them
       alone are non-
            extant

and sonnets always
     have the periodic table
                         cloven gloved and glued
                         mitochondrial blue delve

   housed for anticrystal
observation

  how do your veins
     feel like gales of
yellow clasps
     sorted into individual plastics
for the ripening of divining
         for the source of diving
out wards

there are dives and
     there are these
                         wholespanned by a
                           wakefulness

   that blinds itself
it is sever-al
and all by it selves

two sheets

1

should we stand between two sheets? held at ends? by who knows? and what gum might they be chewing? and where the purple concave tip of your eye? my eye? sagebrush developing wiles? all whiles? what whiles? crushed in house maw? sovereign cow? who deletes the crows? elides the black track of the nautilus? a buried barbed wire? who lives in Hurtsboro? and pulls the pants off the stars? cathexis? cathect? swamp: a dampened red? we dare defend our rights? where do we dare defend our nights? who holds the paint chip you blew on like a snowflake? barter? generator slough and slouch? vulture snap of frugalities? two pages our hands stand between? how's the hollow beard of the fire? buccaneer? cupholder? wound string? cover myself in mucus? make a station of my entrails? ends right? pull the dress from the horizon? and eat? bull landlocked? and the poles are his four heels? bald mission? what hand over that silo? grained? grate of the lips? sifter? not one that is not prologue?

2

The female citherns left rocks beside the road. An artless September heat aligned questions before us like soldiers or robbers. "But the pigeons gather up these traces, gobble them up so that we don't have to," someone said. "Then we must question these pigeons" said another, "or slaughter them if they will not answer, cut them in half and see and taste what oozes or emerges. If not questions then their insides will be our answers." These courses had no effect. Tails of blue disgust followed us like widowers.

    A woman fed me a half-formed baby and my body rang as a bell or rather shook with the pacing of his feet on the ceilings of my skin.

    Most had not actually tried the pigeons. They said they had, wanting to preserve respectability. Courage was paid great lip service. Though only the local cats had taken to the cause with gusto. They received no medals. No little blood trails stained their animistic shirts. Blood cannot be tolerated, even among the courageous.

    Caravans scorched the roads with the impertinent. Engines relaxed for nothing, fed and maintained appropriately. Evening closed each of us in a new room that looked like the old ones. We ran as though hunted. We were hunted. There were those of us who to Astarte, to Persephone, to flea bitten skies, to Yeshua, our bodies framed in sweaters made of splinters, began to repent. And, yes, things were written in the dark. Of these we had imbibed mellifluously as they fell prostrate from our pens. We knew, somehow, the trials we would face could not depose such writing. These phonemes of night cannot be fully grasped in the day. They are moths sitting atop bedposts that would be smashed by the day dwellers who do not understand that they are also the night dwellers.

    Our dreams could not be measured with rulers and though we tried to leave them beneath boulders, they seemed more inclined to drown themselves in water. Some of us decided to spend more time among the water. We told the others we were going to fish. But they became discouraged when we continually returned with so little. We returned less and less. And then, altogether, we stopped.

Sine qua non

worn heels tree cut from shadow barrow
pneumatic
metal beneath rain-corded skin
      soaked in river outpost

barking penumbra split
like prayers between men's fingers

tiny hole between the breasts
bating string spews from it
cut I would make permanent
      to get a hold of
mortis and tenon
      moon pushed into grassy skin

drive her back home
steam rising into mouth's
      downturned cup
stretches a feather so far
      I cannot fly

Howard Hughes
holds his elbows, looks at 8 glasses
      of water rowed
"pine cones may as well be potatoes"
      slow drone cooking
a fable in the marsh

Mezzaluna

And after all this
the bullet does not name you
epact that pulled
   our eye over the horizon

cowering with bells
   talisman stripped of watered whisper
soul drill triangular wall
   into stodgy wave
corporal with fingers in the horse's mouth

       pursed trial peril

tactile meadow:
doorframe and the limen:
subreption of another
       doorframe + limen
body counteracts each of these
       times

            forgive the hatless perjury
            unsolicited shade handles
            wavering stomach trembling
            before each unmemorial
            stray solder of drawer-covered
                lightbands

pulp of lateral garbles
gnomon s-cuff age
      between eyelash swivel
tampering green blades
with flooded stairwells
the caved-in tracks
of our banishments
encased in sea-salt shimmering
      from fuming walls
white outline of a square
windowing on her dress
in the doorway

*

after   even after the tubercular stavings
trees behind which
     the body never hid

*

coronary exultation stitching every
    footstep;
               this did not happen;
drenching drench, drench, wrench
I must be soaked in each moment's
     drowning bag
  soaking over,
         into,
              out of my skin

a pastime, centime

Nasturtium Falls

The water is shivering, the buffaloes all entered, the arcs of their backs become scabs on its skin. The dreaded sacredness...the filter of a house on fire, syrup held bending beneath the nose of a minotaur. What is interred is internment. I do not understand abstraction; it does not exist. Ore despites our manners into unease. What are the axiomatics of nomads? Who has heard them relaying their veins each night under the Catawba? Suicides curdle between and are the crooks of their fingers. Orange moon crows...

Paducah

Each state a preamble
the Ohio River
forgot to write

Indoor swimming pools
we placed seizures of air conditioners
in

Before
the wartraces
had strewn beyond
our darknesses

Driven through at a screaming whisper

Delivering us out of music
and sleep
prismed

Pardoning ourselves for
what we can never pardon ourselves
Buffalo Bill
buried a box of his favorite doughnuts
in that hill
that's now
the city park

The charter

dam falls in love with the water
caresses it like gravel road god leaned on
draws knives like fish to its reticent torso
damn the faces that are shards of barn
sweaters coated in shreds of skin
from parted lips
bellhop
spreads lotion between his hands
diffident smoke upbraids the silverbacked channel
where a tooth fell from the sky
hellblessed
        old parched mint

*

roll up the sleeveblood
finger run through
an orchard sprouting nun's hair
wilddoor that fixed the grey hounding
resembling a reassembling

blue aphid book sewn to your skin
thumbcurtained lichens
like seaflesh trawling itself
for breakwaters long buried

*

mountain is a cold burnt body
an ursine man sweating snow

Marbles will leave you on the stairs

Retribution faces portend fuses
   black stall careens
   a sacredcut shadow building of trees
forceped jewelry delivered
   black canvas
of the paned face
   polemic recrudescence
       is driven to the end of a
nail

simultaneous
   the fingers bleaching
 a white dekagram
             with no end of marooned cheek
               sledge cedar baking a pip
in my nose

the gram of flurry pulled
in like
cocoon seashell dandelion; giving the roses bruise lips
and borrowing
   necklaces from the dirt
sends the icicle narrow
distance into spider bantam
of eye

       white roof thrown under horses' hooves
dental railmen in the limbs
     of the surrogate throat
blue finch dividing his breath
   over the shapes left in the
whalebone battery night

knot nor the banner siphons a street
below yours
   sprain handled music box
billow below be low

    bitrained
          wallow
                  tear
shophan skarp in
  the oval row sur drako
a fill
      decants

Penumbra

grey   lapse

    Sweden   Opel

burrow   zcions
    carnate
arch

        spark fooling the backrow
and the front and the middle

pulling stain-mouthed rabbit
  out of hat
and ladling his paws
  in the corner room of your bifocal mouth
the sun's length a backpulled wedding
  promises
reception for the stars
      a tornado scratched from your navel
and donkeys dead breathing
  annihilating the breast?
not an nihilating but berating the horse throat
the twigs lodged just under the skin:
      alphabet
metacarpal, gradual-turning
slag hands holding purple dress mother
streamed from day's beak

    unduls lating

these separations never in-crease nor de-crease nor separate
    plinths sneaking stone's under each
other's pillow

Dryheel (Pearl)

Benjamin Franklin rolled out of the symbolism buried by Moses in a creek bed:

cemetery has a Ph.D,
is a joiner, hinges rare swells
like lightning's family reunion,
has sewn up a cloak, mummified sky fissures

3 girls wore their faces to school today

the most selfish man is the one who asks for nothing

man with a rectangular eye

mouth is a square deal

the notes are ghost eyes; seeing-eye dogs seeing visions

goats typify bodies which are full of gullets, gills superimposed

there are oven mitts in hell; Proteans in the desert
a child laughs through the door
of who will build the organ: hot air balloon's shadow cast

ground slaps a gorge behind the ear

archaeology blinds us with its bantam tan

your mouth is a square deal squared

oak limbs re-
member a horse hateful men hung
over his association with a hatless farmer

they buried their shoes among the tree's roots

teaspoon of thorns and thrones for the new deal

alchemical model devours socks of
our prostheses

waterfall belt has a red sense
for confessionals, revolvers,
prior priers of our Sophias

our mouth is a square deal

stretching apoplexies in trees

wolves our truck backed over / crushed bone margin
cleft speaking to be spoken

Sister among the bulls

fell down sky-ward

thin buttons, indigo, gold

insertions, apostases between
          men's teeth

stripe that filled your belly

collapse. emboldened pocket of sand

like handful of turtle whiskers
feet disgorge bloodrib

        that pulled your pigtails
when you found artery-stung
dream of crabapple

brushing arm against the warehouse
rubric in the laburnum

Ovum 1

feather bent in two places
were the knuckles in fists

rain dowry
        bleaching your neck
      extending the pine needle
rivulet

uvula portent
encamped over
        windscream tabula

divisions among the roads

cowper sleeves rusted
      to the arms, Ellen,
we threw him by the hair
      steps were indigent waking
quarters of stone
      were halves of our heart

a militia like sand

and what water solves

Ovum 2

encamped feathers
        slide sand in your pockets
retribution, enclosure and a snail
deep inside
eating his own belly

in an old tunnel
        hung the grey mastheads
and father was not in your dream
and were he
        his face would be a cloud of smoke
you will have to make the fissure
with your own hands
        prop open the pointed black beak
with a window
and imagine the sea
the white awning subtends
joined to its inversion

Ovum 4

cattailed vision submerged
        like cornhusk like the bitter

metal frame of your bed
schooling the trailer full of archetype
the station below the swamp
smoke-veined and the leaves
        painted on our forearms

solar foreshadowing
drains set to drain quarantine

the adding on of a detail
of an earring dangled from an eyelid
frozen blue flame, dogsled

        machinations staring from grass
will revere wings
sinking into the long distances of your back

prurient purulent glass broken
        on the shadow-carved tile

palm trees under your bare feet
bracelet is a gift you give
then run away

now it is a full water jug
carried on the shoulder of the one
who accepted it
this will be found and put in
a bag of limbs and torsos
        whose owner
will decorate his house with them

where birds will sing outside
the ocean must fall back into the waterfalls
rocks cannot carve an inch from its face

Robert Hays Segraves

1

```
                        blandishing
                             stone
                        felt for the
                          white halls
                        crowned ditch
swirling stomata
black book
        extending
                        from my chest
graveyards
          mistook                3-toothed
                      among
               trees              mina bird
white veil                       invoking
       the turned brown                    calloused spirits
     [lluvia        lluvial      vial]
                        lets throw them
                            against the second
                                face of the lion



                                buried ring




                                behind his
                                left eye
                                turning sea graves
```

2

```
memory curving around your face
           do not apprehend him
           the two-eyed I
           surfaces umbrelled in each
                                new air
portunate onion        prefatal starch
         haired
                             venal winds
                             we carried
                                 filmed and
```

        sealed

    false shoe
        diamonding
     my hand
the silver cord

 greeting
like snail pressing
      against my nose
triple column
   straining even more
the building long gone
     frozen echo
 etched into the
shape of his ears
cyclops dwindling
  not to mention love
griot
      ogre of cardinal
 pointed against
   the leaves
away from the barrow
crushed grape
     and toe like ladle

3

   (wristfork

4

        whithering beetle
     training his scream
      on the unilegged mountain
his beak maligned as a key

carves unseen harbors
                in the titled lands

do I have a wing
        or is my coat only half-on?

the winding shoe
            stuck in the loose pockets
        folded in the written dust
    stables underfed in the coral sealed
                gymnasiums
            ballooned paroxysm
tableau we must refrain from
            empty chairs
unfilled spaces
        re-capillary
    the lungs' imagination
implement of forebreath
        crowbar of afterbreath
    genuine stealth pimpled
        in foam studded rapid
    water of sound done away with

                away done sound

apse lit with darkness
            checkered doornail beaten out
                of the face
rotting polaroids do not limbo
    in the chest that streams
            undiscounted
whittling of holes
            mine of days

Afterword

Barge hung from god's neck
nibbles baritone spickets
in-spouts the brittle mouth
that boy called your heart:
    first fencepost,
swilled pecan shells
in water cold davenport

grandmother kneel:
    a collarbone and your yoke

grandfather kneel:
    a man only cries bottles with
        nothing inside

penance pries an old bugle,
silver, officious prelate
tasting the weather of raw crayfish

exposure is ever-dental,
    evidential
when balled like black stockings:

wind hanging from god's neck
    like gods,
war species' circles
shredded into metallic hairstrands

sunken bridge of the nose
drillbit that is your estuary

reconciles a disease called
    cosmos
darkening in the sun

darken a prayer like beetroot

an get what you

room made of doors
        will always turn
                side ways

blasphemy is a thief who
holds his boyhood pains
in the corpses of his thumbs

corpse tilts a bucket of jaundiced
        cherries and drinks them
into a sun

charred fecal nail
delineates aviary stream's
avatar: volition

Parnassus show and tells a clay
ribbon with no bottom

axle of revelation
casting long shadow
always back, doubling

double back

an get what you

minnows petrify into a
        curtain and
sleeve a docile farewell

        grandmother

not among buttons pressed
        mantleward
by inscrutable eyetanks--

deaspect the quarry limbed in
volume of a beggar's tree

saw the breakwater into
an amphibious saddle
bilious deployment
shrieks a window sticky

with apple juice pall

suture projects a fin
that is Mars' left lung
hanging low in the sky

it looks green even to those who know
better

what virgin mallets
sleep beneath their own husks

calling a telephone
meant to be an arm
table kneeling over a crater

an get what you

grandfather grandmother

—horse skull was a house
a willow put a knife to

as a dove's tail

bog became a yellow wall
after I turned to it
as a lover

burned blackberries breathed
       as nipples

I covered the bowel
       of cilia's scratch paper

Give it a name
full of anger
a horse's name
anagrammed

Beth-Salem

  North about
death licentiate
  Decembermoved
    chestaught in
       eldersmiles'
Wilderness
                Hannah
Later-   Sarah
  Chain   Martha
  minister   Maria
Jewelled
artery century

aria is sentient

[an overlapping]

an overlapping
that could break the hollow spell of a cup
strands of hair placed in the spinner's cooling glass
I had borne you on the leaf edges of my teeth
but to only swallow gardens
or a warm pie left on a dirt road
there were wells lit like canopies
but not a diver
devotion in mercy's closeheld divot

[an analogical patience]

an analogical patience
anarchical
to wait
handful of raisins
baptism framed in font of surgeon's tools
sweaty foot held between legs maternal
matins
a coastal hearing
floating judges
how they are sick
of wind
of sea
lead pipe spawning mud sky
held on rust-colored wings
and bones of songs
ride early
before the clovers' morning aspersion
diaretic
leaf unswerving
into the fairground hilt
strings of shallow pink paper
are the waning outward orifice
somatic peeling undereye
under I
shallots have carried away the beaks
that swallowed their own ravens
identifyed
dyed in the light
of shouldered altar

[binding of the mouth freelances...]

binding of the mouth freelances
undernight
pearl-bathed, sour-lipped
beray a flashing flesh
spasm everreframing
father and mother
taste their milled dew
letterwash the slow vanishing
no shape
make a conjurer silled
snow only caught in arboreal orifices
not ground touching
labor is arachnid
adooring

Stethoscope in Garden

In your mouth the black buttons
fur's supplication is never
to be left on the ground

Hortense   arms crumpling back into her stomach
ripe old sanctuary indawned
a resinous flirtation

the community bank still divided into stalls:
air rupturing octaves of horses

do the conch dance
with a mouthful of berries,
winter's gravel

the barnyard has a visor
a wish covering its face
a page stung with flattened beads

you read the book through the blood of your murders
in all likelihood

*

marzipan diamond holds the ritual line of snow
wild fortifications of the nipple

that expanse curd farmer Jesse
would draw his saw across
if he had a limbic system
or could wield a primary color

like an eyebrow,
canopy of sutured ribbons:
adornment for the war

*

the Lord has a sin he will wall up the town with

watches the well of rain-soaked noodles
the turion arc from its cover
night slobbering over its bleeding bags of fire
white-eyed coverlets,
hair mashed in nail file mortar

five o'clock has an intercom
a burst-loined even voice
the loudspeaker mummified in plastic bleached shadows,
flags of the flood

trees make a tribal web,
fallen forest:
a woman with a mailbox
and no house
the white mollusk girl circles
on her bike

"until the flood,"
the woman greets her
her rapture carved from the ground
that is falling from her feet

*

violet-shouldered Wahab,
a flower held between his shoulder blades,
makes a northward turn

the arctic   he knows   always curves
the salvage of the liable

Copy of *Silas Marner*

The jagged words we put in
arches of our feet
trade for the blue-limbed
jungle canopy of the car
you were born under
not our words
not our bodies

surely the archdiocese
will stop holding raffles
for gilded baby's fingers

watch your image rise in hollow
lung balcony of
nine women who buried themselves
in a bowl of rusted jelly beans
beggars spit their teeth in

who rent himself with a jagged board
brain matter strung on clothes lines
beaten the breath out of
like the word you could
only say in your sleep
something with an f and s

you would trade us for words
our words
whining about death like
rubber snakes
regime's hat
caught in racimes
the period actually a decimal
courting windings in nunneries

I understood love
only like an old bicycle
two wheels spinning

some old whitewashed wind

but with what jagged board did
you cleave the first?

fabric too brittle for wind
becomes wind

there are fat-laced soaps
and hot and cold water
an eyeline we must walk along
until we can no longer be seen

burial knocks at the door
when we pardon it
wants to know if it can look at our magazines

Silver changes hands

antiphon and reichstag
dug out a cradle in the floor
of their new apartment
filled it with hay

dripped blue quill fever labor
headstone of heaven

vortex of arms waving
kneading the ocean's
carbines yodeling outside
seasons

foredawned curve marked their pillows
skull-encased millstone
bed as metaphor
phosphorescent scene of
a station east of here
out of earshot

industry is the bulging of
words' mouths

drawn into a brown-eyed voice
a man leaves a cotton fire to its barn
sticks gum on antiphon's
underarm
finger pressed in blind
utricle of reichstag's chest

bread crumbs weep
per-spire   rant
resting in lion's white mane

table settings become breasts
for us to sleep at

teeth carved cathedral ceilings
in mouths

this is where war comes in
to show his home movies:

his little girl doing
rhythmic gymnastics
his father slow-drifting to
the bottom of the sea
through his wonder at what
brought him back

after he leaves
they decide to lathe
an image, a body
but this changes
it is none of their business

War

You should not drink my blood
it will only upset your stomach
lower intestine
        is your best friend
not excepting everyone else
who fooled you into thinking those
  little white pieces of paper were
their teeth

shinbones hung from the telephone wires
make smoke spume from your
right eye—
radiator

deviant proposition all are
even the ones that bite us where we want
even the ones with hooks we know
even they have distant cousins
who carry sharpened bits of slate
        in their socks
who used to have a dog

and they should come over
        some time
          of
                course

Open window

Keep waiting for the storm
to drag you up
    the basement stairs

doing anything is a matter of time
he's an insurance claims specialist
can represent you
hassle free
          from beginning till end

hail can shatter windows
                    but not lost lives

drop on milk cold floor
batons in the hands
fallow heart spitting out
      names of his old wife
who held her nose
   in the crease
      of his
right arm right side

I hear an animal that is not singing

water spiders lead me into my yet to be worn wake
how can anyone think in water

every one knows
dead or alive
the water changes your body

voices are distances
body cannot help but ask
if martyr matters more

when you realize your fingers are shells
the air wraps its knees around you
you know you're about
to die

a shock like any other
but without the rest of your life
to feed and clothe it

A snowfire not born(e) again

1

The walking sticks decide to gather under the oaks
they hiss when the catcher from the Tongie Reds
sets them on fire
you sing God Has Spared Me a Name Even He Cannot Read
you sing Hallelujah The Dreams Have Come to Enlist Me

last night someone superglued quarters over every lock downtown
a reminder to look at the moon

the gasoline left in the mower has boiled out your love
the water shadows building at our pockets
full of the ice cubes we used to smash blood bugs
you sing The Night is a Wart in the Zebra's Eye
you sing That Old Cocker Spaniel Bit My Mother
you sing Let Me Be Embroidered in Sweat Bees When I Die Oh Lord

*

mother wears a headdress
your father had a headdress for her
of Black Cats and Ace Combs

*

some night you will have a thin worry
wrapped like vellum over your skin
wonder what to write since it only winds
around your body

so you become a sideshow in a snowdrift
the kissing booth might as well
go casting for minnows
the hawk beak your mother cradled in her arms
like a map's legend

where the divine way becomes the human
—at your head?—
they threw a styrofoam cup
you picked it up
realized you were calling your name
and are marked absent
your mother will later contest this

*

"I've got a hard-on so hard it's giving me a headache"
thinking of the nymphs, currents
that were supposed to flow over us
Mother, I can smell the demon, his heart
open like a giant oak
pressing knife to Isis
to every bone in our bodies
he spit his gum in my soup
ate all my Captain's Wafers
he took a child bride once, took her to the woods
and when she got older he cut open her body
and climbed in to what no one remembered and
for a while he was married to the man with black marbles
in his ears: herder of every dying word
runs Kelly's Sportsbar and Family Restaurant
is the first base coach for the Tongie Reds
the fools at the state fair tried to hire him
once as the Man Who Could Hear the Future—
island littered with broken eyeglasses—
"get out the old spectaculars grandpa,
the abacus strung with blue fish skeletons shines like lightning"
his wife died when she threw up three Grade A chicken eggs
shells intact that no one would touch
except the man with black marbles in his ears's son
whose pickup they found stranded in a field
doors left open like the wings of a dead bird
no one ever heard him again
though I could swear I once heard some blood singing
in the airplane fuselage behind my grandfather's house

*

The demon spent the night in his mother's arms. Creation had always repulsed him. The volitions involved, scouring over the hardened rock of phlegm that held the pulse of his anger. This pulse he prized so long as its assessment lay fallow.

He had seen a priest at the behest of his mother (doting). The man had made him hot-seasoned pork chops. And they ate under the waxed car hoods of a magnolia's leaves; the bones they had strewn into effigies of each other, the demon used an empty whisky bottle as a phallus for the priest's. A dog came by and licked them both around the elbows and faces. And the priest spoke (mostly):
   —Detriment.
   —Why?
   —A pagan shadow shall cast among the lambs, the full milk raised from the carved hide of the bull. Do you believe in its retribution? The sky's mask. Or carry a walnut hidden under your beard. The finest man and/or woman I ever knew sat mostly on an overturned bucket and held up cherries to her eyes. The reddest fable did not comb her hair each day nor leave a light on in her house. She gave a rose to the escarpment that pulled itself on top of that hill. The wall strains just as you do and the cemetery has no windows or doors. The sexton may sing from the night of his hunger but he does not pull the wings off of horse-angels. Have some more whisky. The detriment has gripped me below the raiment these past 600 years and the marker of my chin leads dogs to the whimpering of trees. Do not juxtapose flight and compassion, the hard shell bleeds the standard river in which wades the diminutive feet; these extend trails through silt that only a hawk could see and only momentarily like the vibration of a perfectly still doorknob. The amputee does not frame the severed leg nor the severed leg frame him; a microphone undetectable in his pocket will give you an abscess the size of a mountain quarried with penknives and splintered fingernails. If you suckle from them (the fingernails not the penknives), the liquid issuing would be as the terrain of a bonfire in which giant worms have burned under the awnings of dolmen and strung cut-out airplanes and snowflakes above the aboriginal heart.
   —Where will I find this?

—Plumed from the starchy bosom that grazed the thousands or more men like me in the fallen tower of the orchard in autumn. Things will seem to scratch and stream from your whiskers and will be as ants that swallow bits of flesh from the head of the dead brown thrush. You can see his cousin if you bring him a butterfly perched on a silver ring. These are not the customs I made but one has to keep a shoehold over the cliff of the chest.

—This is what I have been saying.

—Wrong. This is what you have not been saying. This is what has acted as a bite that swallows your entire body, leaving the indentation to the eyes of old weavers and stocky magicians with broad-brimmed noses. Noses smell for waves when the waves are noses. Picking mold from the wax seals graves a spooled stick from the breast of a man; and the relapse approves the original lapse by negating it, by burying the old latticed bench to flail a bag of apple seeds above your head. The old straggler lapse is the bacon, fried and eaten, birthing a slow growing shadow that fills with your indentation, your body prodded with grey stork beaks.

—Do I have a balm?

—The strangest reflection commandeers a raised tug of skin. Do we receive the foreshadowing when the moon picks a sickle and breaks it over the machete of night's forebearances. The equivocal soldier spreads his lunch out on the ground to find a magnifying glass held between his palm and sandwich. The birds sing and a catbite overwhelms his bating in the recrudescence of wet sheep's wool. The clothes in which you have garnished me give me a light from sparrow's eyes but it is so small and you are too far away to see it. I have given my daughter over to a man who welds under a syrupy falls of black tar but he gives the window his every breath and lays his shirts out after the days have ended. This dust will never touch his lips and molten river streams over him to the point of a seafought triangle. The violence spelled in each of his words has to outweigh the thick film of his existence. We are men of air and the rain is a falling curtain of vines, blinds that little arrogances pivot around like dogs. This man can see nothing and his words must be honestly culled if they are to bubble through to the stomach of my blackened daughter.

—And the collapse? What if it has me?

—It does. But we must sweat to the accordion of our birthdeath. Bones crack in the exposed air and we place the little bits inside. Fire is a man's only true barber.

*

you dip your shirt in the stream
this is calling your father
the man with black bruise on his nose that never healed
he grew a beard
and like the ocean your mother never liked it
she said the high rollers all move to the desert
and try to drink off the mud-dark
ricochets of their bodies

a woman lays on her stomach
on a high oak branch
and proceeds to cut every hair off her head
as you lay below
and imagine that the falling locks are only
feathers covering your face
and that they will use the giraffes and chains
to draw the drowned cupboard out of the lake
and then you think of the molars
they had to knock out on either side of the giraffes' mouths
for those chains
the indentations that will have to be made
will have to be made you think
in the wind and blood-feud whistling

2

shop of what blood
would be held in their hands
swum wild in snowdrift spine
captured child marooned
from the Ming Dynasty
the wallpaper grew from a flower
nailed to the wall

each day
each day
is
landing

*

drainage ditch overflowed with splinter
soup from Pilate's wood stove—
automated—carbuncular—
raisin toast dropped in briars
bronze buckle Rhine belt clawed out window's
continental flank for your barest bones
—enclaves—fisher of drawers
for lighthouse sepulchre milieu
oven mitt for the emperor
I didn't mean (?)
I was being heraldic
seer making children's drawings
from crayon-filled horse entrails
arch rivals pin candy wrappers to the wall
recarving the melted wax box for cowardice
matriculations
matrimonial
a snowfire not born again

*

they are drilling below the gloved fingers
mitred
    stashed
        in the cardroom of the palfrey
that held the coiffure, blackwhite dress
gesture that held your mother
until it rained snow
she could stow into the umber moons
of her underarms

cholera held the man conduit
the lead blue porpoise
she touched
cold windows of her hands
in order to breathe better
the letter
long cataloging the breast
dipped in iodine
weld fleece to two is
always rifling

*

bent wing sail
Spanish Armada sold
for the right priest
who always holds a silver case
full with gauze
he tries to wrap around the tide

spider wrestles through the feathers
of the peacock
who would tolerate this:
a wooden river
that he could parade across
and down and up
the village all drinking cider
and whispering
about the con-
stitutional
the leathery hide that wanders
at night through interstices of alleys
of weather-knotted pitchers
old stucco flecked in
undulant billing
between ghosts growing naked
in the outcropping of their own hair
clover shedding like their whetted whetting

*

cart the nails to the sky
idle the welded wagon
moss' missive
barn-widowed light
like the bleached extension cord
wound over the coil
of the mouse's tail

wife leaves   where your finger
records   left the linen
shame into   black markets
a lithe story   bookish scales
weathering the word   glowering
where the word is   sold
weathered whethering
the black shooting star
hidden from the sight of God

Photograph of silo and Nora Leintz

  nude of heavy material   careening offhand
  as frieze
  or altar   handoff
  spread breath siphoning questions like sleeping
    crawfish   wound
  music preformed offhand   solar helter
    dims lips   knifing Dionysus
                              in blue jeans
                              and alterity
                              ice nesting
                              in its own sides
                              flanks are tonal
                              blind willowing into
                                excerpts
                              gnarled cupholders
                              culled from Lancelot's
                                reputed armor
                              be leveling
                              a history
                              into the cottony nitrous
                              throwing yourself
                              against earlier blue
                                impasse, backyard
                              of later blue
                    strange: a man named Arkwright
                        invented the spinning (water) frame:
                            the chartable quiet
              invents the charting of quiet

Ensiform

barrier reef slain into extensions
exiting
finally
the man falls sideways
knows something of the recognition
that bleaches anguish
into a toothsome incision

arm was there and there
          and there
there the white bricks

pockmarks angels left on my ears
singing
like holding a buck knife
out the car window

and condensing the air
to one gut-whale point

[Artifact]

Artifacts   the human dead

art affects the human dead

ecclesiastical   the nominative spleen ordains your arteries
     spread with blue fingers   spread with blue fingers
                                                                         hoist
          the Arno

the machinations given gums stretched into shape of eyelids
        gargle Hell's waters and the old fetus flown against your
Mithraic heart

Tauroctony   Flood   Tauroctony   Flood

art's effect   the human dead

Place de la Révolution

eulogy thought
or place of a conduit called
hyperion
         daggerhold i   bury in heck of natives   the fourth of four in

io folds the cropper verticall like hull curve like rain
infects (inflects) its the hardest hold on yourbody clean sock and a
rock of each
   remonstrative toe
                           and carrion on the old hovering caresill
      halved letters half placed in the future

                                  endearing if only
white bull-lion asked along the corridor —rinse them old he-arts
like washing a child in the river when we are all dangling limbs
from limbs

Dehiscence

alloutward   hell's shale   all shells
only have outsides when
to write—nauticalize—
as: to do with concretive nations
same to die

        as to have claimed to spit on a narwhal
you the ocean/upswung arms to shelter distance   hold it
                              in place

                                      —my swords
but have you swung upon yourself today. I'm the leaf man I seep
canyons sweep them from the church rectory not long now in the
instant you were born. Hider of the spare staples not only a belletrist
but a conjoined twin of the harpsichord leftist. The whole pile of
blood has a judicial effect not only splitting hairs but braiding them
slid through cracks in doors until I must tell you about hinges...

—I could not carry spume of a comet over river
not for even under a centimeter since
each time is as a/has a trimester   involuted

—put your hands in your pockets
it's cold

Dear _____

unter-
ikon   pacific
in the nadir the eye
round to throwing a tennis shoe blasted phlegm myth
or in the andes shivering like the night
the horses ingest gently
however you like the world ironed out before
when they put a piece of cardboard in the crux between each your
fingers
and ask you now   to worry about them

Herr Night blows the dinner whistle

Nigel has the father complex
all confers in the wink of his moustache the way paintings have focal
    points
in spite of which they reprise all the arched back of the earth
not to go to lengths not at all to go to lengths but the roundest route
    has the shortest
breath and this has us out of our boxers and reengendering the
    pubescence of leaves the
refrigerator is a knight armored in white
and how to keep the severed
horizon lines whose secrets we whispered when locked inside it
when there's a drawing for an open-faced sandwich then call me
until isolated grocery stores have a brittle bark
that steppes like rising water
forearm of her throat's carnality
refrigerator is a night armored in white

The work of night is coming

not wholly vestigial
when a choir is not a choir

always always always always

the way all rigid tight-furnished reflections in windows of quinceañera

the maxim farmer has wielded his breath into the ornate C of his
horse's shoes

walk a piece or a place in his shoes or a place walk a piece
in my shoes

tow what is fornicatable behind like the seven breasts whole
swallowed before we ever
got beyond the mailbox

spice-rack filled with handguns

marks us as oceanic travesties swilled in the back of our father's
throats "how to will oneself into that old courthouse" "the state fair's
next week" "the red skin of that rhinoceros's eye like to murdered me
into senility" "not to be a bother but could you see to it

after Adrienne Rich

until now we only allow thoughts to walk
back to back
everything turns out to be foraging
and voice
these supplant time and distance

—thoughts of which until-now—
how my mother wrung milk from your hair
and guided my hand, brushed it with
my hand
the only place less unfashioned
knowing your motion
can be a-
way

If I could tell you how to isolate things

I could tell you if I could tell who isolated things how they isolated things the legerdemain whisper the facts to Old Cashew Ears how to shoot the river spin oats in the breeze to touch every hair's tongue tip light outlights the rusty squibs torched in the basement of the baseball card store to quit fields into quiltfields who could have isolated things love coming in with the language WITH THE LANGUAGE! and swim around the heads ringed with flowers bobbing in the river keep swimming and scoring the water with our bodies to tell how to isolate things words heavylight limbs of forgetting Quitanos sparrows that got caught in basketball nets Fear's gnarled cuticles "I shot the river" just before I put my face to the warm small of its back and it wiped its muzzle on me I could feel its legs pushing beneath me sound menacing the Sound of meaning wolves gave all their kindnesses to its creeks the water drinks itself dry tries to conjugate itself suckles at inflections of bog oak roots undertow has the sound of jackrabbits breathing shy borders themselves themselves breathing hierarchy vorstellung happy to be in the first room of the first house behind the first door that ever reconsidered the sad smile of your belly that ever reconsidered how to tell you to isolate things to put your hands into splinters into shadowangles of things if it knew if I knew I would tell anyone how to isolate things anyone only you could know

Matthew Goethe is a poet living in Atlanta, GA. Many of his poems have appeared in half-finished notebooks and on loose bits of paper. Though completed over ten years ago, *A Snowfire Not Born(e) Again* is his first collection of poems to be published in book form. Alternate versions of some of these poems can be found in his sound work as Double Vanities on the album *How Come Your Sister Doesn't Know My Name Anymore*, also released by Sweet Wreath.

www.ingramcontent.com/pod-product-compliance
Lightning Source LLC
Chambersburg PA
CBHW022120090426
42743CB00008B/942